Table of Conter*

I . Addition

    1 . Learn Addition

    2 . Practice Problems with differnt methods

    3 . Addition Word Problems

II . Subtraction

    1 . Learn Subtraction

    2 . Practice Problems with differnt methods

    3 . Subtraction Word Problems

III . Mixed Addition and Subtraction

IV . Comparing Numbers

V . Geometry

Addition

On a sheet of paper, draw 4 dots, then draw 3 more dots next to the first 4.

1. How many dots did you draw initially?

_____

2. How many more dots did you draw next to the first ones?

_____

3. If you count all the dots you have drawn, what is the total?

_____

4. Can you write the corresponding addition to show how you found the total?

_____

5. So, how many dots are there now?

_____

Learn Addition

$1 + 2 = 3$

$1 + 1 = 2$

$2 + 2 = 4$

$2 + 0 = 2$

$3 + 2 = 5$

$3 + 3 = 6$

Learn Addition

$$4 + 3 = 7$$

$$5 + 1 = 6$$

$$5 + 4 = 9$$

$$0 + 3 = 3$$

$$4 + 4 = 8$$

$$7 + 3 = 10$$

Count and Add

Count and Add

```
☐ + ☐ = ☐          ☐ + ☐ = ☐

☐ + ☐ = ☐          ☐ + ☐ = ☐

☐ + ☐ = ☐          ☐ + ☐ = ☐
```

Count and Add

0
+ 5 ●●●●●
_____
- - - - - -
_____

3 ●●●
+ 2 ●●
_____
- - - - - -
_____

4 ●●●●
+ 3 ●●●
_____
- - - - - -
_____

5 ●●●●●
+ 3 ●●●
_____
- - - - - -
_____

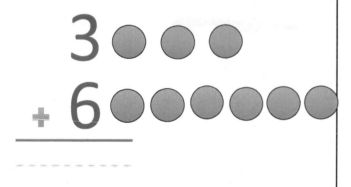

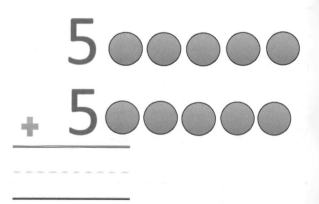

Count and Add

3 ●●●
+ 3 ●●●
_____

3 ●●●
+ 2 ●●
_____

4 ●●●●
+ 2 ●●
_____

5 ●●●●●
+ 2 ●●
_____

4 ●●●●
+ 6 ●●●●●●
_____

5 ●●●●●
+ 4 ●●●●
_____

Write the answer

$2 + 3 = \boxed{}$

$2 + 8 = \boxed{}$

$5 + 3 = \boxed{}$

$3 + 4 = \boxed{}$

$4 + 0 = \boxed{}$

$6 + 3 = \boxed{}$

Write the answer

$9 + 0 = \boxed{}$

$4 + 4 = \boxed{}$

$5 + 5 = \boxed{}$

$7 + 1 = \boxed{}$

$4 + 5 = \boxed{}$

$6 + 4 = \boxed{}$

Write the answer

3 + 3 ———	7 + 2 ———
4 + 6 ———	7 + 1 ———
3 + 4 ———	6 + 2 ———

Write the answer

$$8$$
$$+\ 2$$
_____

$$5$$
$$+\ 2$$
_____

$$3$$
$$+\ 6$$
_____

$$7$$
$$+\ 3$$
_____

$$2$$
$$+\ 2$$
_____

$$6$$
$$+\ 1$$
_____

To make **5 stars**, we can have

★   ★ ★ ★ ★

$1 + 4 = 5$ stars

★ ★   ★ ★ ★

$2 + 3 = 5$ stars

Now, let's think of three other ways
to make a group of **5 stars**

☐ + ☐	=	5
☐ + ☐	=	5
☐ + ☐	=	5

To make **6 oranges**, we can have

$$2 + 4 = 6 \text{ oranges}$$

$$3 + 3 = 6 \text{ oranges}$$

Now, let's think of three other ways to make a group of **6 oranges**

☐ + ☐	=	6
☐ + ☐	=	6
☐ + ☐	=	6

To make **7 cats**, we can have

$$3 + 4 = 7 \text{ cats}$$

$$6 + 1 = 7 \text{ cats}$$

Now, let's think of three other ways to make a group of **7 cats**

☐ + ☐	=	7
☐ + ☐	=	7
☐ + ☐	=	7

To make **8 bananas**, we can have

4 + 4 = 8 bananas

5 + 3 = 8 bananas

Now, let's think of three other ways

to make a group of **8 bananas**

☐ + ☐	=	8
☐ + ☐	=	8
☐ + ☐	=	8

To make 9 **Butterflies**, we can have

7 + 2 = 9 butterflies

3 + 6 = 9 butterflies

Now, let's think of three other ways

to make a group of 9 **Butterflies**

☐	+	☐	=	9
☐	+	☐	=	9
☐	+	☐	=	9

To make 10 hearts, we can have

$$6 + 4 = 10 \text{ hearts}$$

$$2 + 8 = 10 \text{ hearts}$$

Now, let's think of three other ways to make a group of 10 hearts

☐	+ ☐	=	10
☐	+ ☐	=	10
☐	+ ☐	=	10

Fill in the missing number

$2 + \boxed{} = 8$ $3 + \boxed{} = 7$

$5 + \boxed{} = 9$ $\boxed{} + 4 = 10$

$4 + \boxed{} = 4$ $1 + \boxed{} = 9$

Fill in the missing number

$5 + \boxed{} = 10$ $8 + \boxed{} = 10$

$6 + \boxed{} = 9$ $\boxed{} + 0 = 2$

$3 + \boxed{} = 6$ $4 + \boxed{} = 8$

Fill in the missing number

$7 + \boxed{} = 10$

$8 + \boxed{} = 8$

$1 + \boxed{} = 9$

$0 + \boxed{} = 2$

$2 + \boxed{} = 6$

$4 + \boxed{} = 9$

Fill in the missing number

$\boxed{} + \boxed{2} = \boxed{9}$

$\boxed{} + \boxed{1} = \boxed{6}$

$\boxed{} + \boxed{5} = \boxed{10}$

$\boxed{} + \boxed{3} = \boxed{3}$

$\boxed{} + \boxed{1} = \boxed{10}$

$\boxed{} + \boxed{3} = \boxed{7}$

Read and solve the problems

Michael has four apples and William has three apples. How many apples do Michael and William have together?

_____ + _____ = _____

There are five small balls and four big balls. How many balls are there altogether?

_____ + _____ = _____

Read and solve the problems

Five tomatoes are in the basket. Five
more tomatoes are put in the basket.
How many tomatoes are in the basket
now?

_____ + _____ = _____

There are eight small oranges and two
big oranges. How many oranges are
there altogether?

_____ + _____ = _____

Read and solve the problems

Three bananas are in the basket. six more bananas are put in the basket. How many bananas are in the basket now?

_____ + _____ = _____

James has seven more cherries than William. William has two cherries. How many cherries does James have?

_____ + _____ = _____

Read and solve the problems

James has four more oranges than William. William has three oranges. How many oranges does James have?

_____ + _____ = _____

Michael has five more apples than James. James has three apples. How many apples does Michael have?

_____ + _____ = _____

Subtraction

On a sheet of paper, draw 7 dots. Then, cross out 3 of these dots with a pen or pencil.

1. How many dots did you draw initially?

_____

2. How many dots did you cross out?

_____

3. If you count the dots that are not crossed out, how many are there left?

_____

4. Can you write the corresponding subtraction to show how you found the number of uncrossed dots?

_____

5. So, how many uncrossed dots are there now on the paper?

_____

Learn Subtraction

2 - 1 = 1

3 - 1 = 2

4 - 2 = 2

4 - 3 = 1

5 - 3 = 2

6 - 1 = 5

Learn Subtraction

5 - 2 = 3

6 - 3 = 3

6 - 5 = 1

7 - 3 = 4

9 - 4 = 5

10 - 3 = 7

Count and Subtract

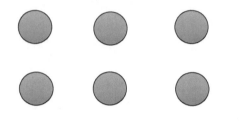

6 - 1 = ☐   6 - 2 = ☐

7 - 3 = ☐   8 - 4 = ☐

9 - 2 = ☐   10 - 5 = ☐

Count and Subtract

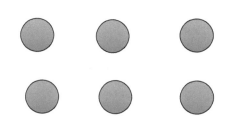

6 - 3 = ☐

6 - 5 = ☐

7 - 4 = ☐

8 - 1 = ☐

9 - 6 = ☐

10 - 7 = ☐

Count and Subtract

5 $-\ 1$ _____ _____	6 $-\ 2$ _____ _____
8 $-\ 3$ _____ _____	10 $-\ 2$ _____ _____
7 $-\ 4$ _____ _____	8 $-\ 5$ _____ _____

Count and Subtract

5
- 3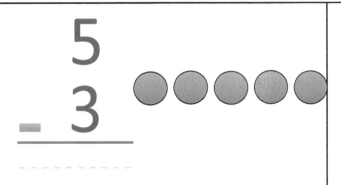
_____
......
_____

6
- 5
_____
......
_____

8
- 1
_____
......
_____

10
- 6
_____
......
_____

7
- 0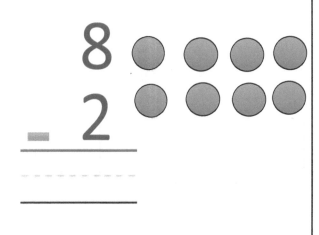
_____
......
_____

8
- 2
_____
......
_____

Write the answer

$3 - 2 = \boxed{}$

$4 - 1 = \boxed{}$

$1 - 1 = \boxed{}$

$3 - 0 = \boxed{}$

$5 - 2 = \boxed{}$

$5 - 4 = \boxed{}$

Write the answer

$6 - 4 = \boxed{}$ $7 - 5 = \boxed{}$

$8 - 1 = \boxed{}$ $8 - 7 = \boxed{}$

$9 - 3 = \boxed{}$ $10 - 4 = \boxed{}$

Write the answer

5 − 3 ———— — — — ————	6 − 1 ———— — — — ————
1 − 0 ———— — — — ————	10 − 3 ———— — — — ————
7 − 6 ———— — — — ————	8 − 3 ———— — — — ————

Write the answer

4 − 3 ─────	5 − 1 ─────
9 − 7 ─────	10 − 6 ─────
7 − 7 ─────	8 − 5 ─────

To make **5 stars**, we can have

★ ★ ★ ★ ★ ✹

6 - 1 = 5 stars

★ ★ ★ ★ ★ ✹ ✹ ✹ ✹

9 - 4 = 5 stars

Now, let's think of three other ways
to make a group of **5 stars**

☐	- ☐	=	5
☐	- ☐	=	5
☐	- ☐	=	5

To make **6 Balls**, we can have

8 - 2 = 6 Balls

Now, let's think of three other ways
to make a group of **6 Balls**

☐	-	☐	=	6
☐	-	☐	=	6
☐	-	☐	=	6

Think of three ways to make a group of 7 apples

	−		=	7
	−		=	7
	−		=	7

Fill in the missing number

$5 - \boxed{} = 2$ $3 - \boxed{} = 1$

$1 - \boxed{} = 0$ $4 - \boxed{} = 1$

$5 - \boxed{} = 4$ $4 - \boxed{} = 2$

Fill in the missing number

8 - ☐ = 3

7 - ☐ = 4

9 - ☐ = 1

10 - ☐ = 3

5 - ☐ = 0

7 - ☐ = 1

Fill in the missing number

☐ - 3 = 1	☐ - 3 = 2
☐ - 4 = 0	☐ - 1 = 4
☐ - 3 = 5	☐ - 2 = 3

Fill in the missing number

$\boxed{} - \boxed{1} = \boxed{8}$ $\boxed{} - \boxed{3} = \boxed{6}$

$\boxed{} - \boxed{7} = \boxed{2}$ $\boxed{} - \boxed{5} = \boxed{5}$

$\boxed{} - \boxed{3} = \boxed{7}$ $\boxed{} - \boxed{5} = \boxed{3}$

Read and solve the problems

William has three balls. Then William gives two balls to Michael. How many balls does William have left now?

_____ − _____ = _____

Six apples are on the table. Then James bumps into the table, and three apples fall off. How many apples are left on the table now?

_____ − _____ = _____

Read and solve the problems

James has five fewer pens than William. William has eight pens. How many pens does James have?

_____ - _____ = _____

Seven balls are in the basket. Three are red and the rest are green. How many balls are green?

_____ - _____ = _____

Read and solve the problems

10 pens are in the backpack. Four are red and the rest are green. How many pens are green?

_____ — _____ = _____

Michael has 4 fewer oranges than William. William has 6 oranges. How many oranges does Michael have?

_____ — _____ = _____

Read and solve the problems

7 balls are in the basket. Three are red and the rest are green. How many balls are green?

_____ - _____ = _____

Michael has seven fewer oranges than James. James has 10 oranges. How many oranges does Michael have?

_____ - _____ = _____

Mixed Problems
Addition and
Subtraction

Write the answer

1 + 3 - 2 = ☐

4 - 1 + 5 = ☐

3 + 0 - 2 = ☐

4 - 2 + 3 = ☐

3 - 3 + 3 = ☐

4 + 1 - 5 = ☐

Write the answer

5 + 3 - 2 = ☐

4 - 3 + 7 = ☐

9 + 0 - 3 = ☐

8 - 2 + 4 = ☐

7 - 3 + 5 = ☐

8 + 1 - 4 = ☐

Write the answer

6	+	3	-	1	=	

5	-	2	+	7	=	

4	+	0	-	3	=	

8	-	7	+	5	=	

4	-	3	+	8	=	

6	+	4	-	2	=	

Write the answer

7	+	3	-	8	=	

10	-	5	+	4	=	

3	+	5	-	8	=	

8	-	2	+	4	=	

9	-	9	+	9	=	

8	+	1	-	6	=	

Write the answer

5 - 3 - 2 = ☐

8 - 3 - 4 = ☐

9 - 3 - 3 = ☐

8 - 2 - 5 = ☐

10 - 3 - 5 = ☐

8 - 0 - 8 = ☐

Write the answer

$1 + 4 - 3 + 2 = \boxed{}$

$3 - 1 + 5 - 4 = \boxed{}$

$6 + 4 - 3 - 7 = \boxed{}$

$5 - 5 + 5 + 1 = \boxed{}$

$4 + 3 + 2 - 8 = \boxed{}$

$8 - 2 - 3 + 4 = \boxed{}$

Write the answer

5	+	2	-	3	+	4	=	
6	-	3	+	5	-	6	=	
7	+	2	-	3	-	4	=	
9	-	5	+	3	+	2	=	
3	+	5	+	2	-	7	=	
9	-	2	-	3	+	1	=	

Write the answer

6 + 2 - 3 + 4 = ☐

7 - 3 + 2 - 5 = ☐

5 + 2 - 3 - 4 = ☐

9 - 5 + 1 + 5 = ☐

3 + 3 + 3 - 7 = ☐

9 - 4 - 5 + 9 = ☐

Write the answer

$7 + 2 - 4 + 5 = \boxed{}$

$5 - 5 + 5 - 5 = \boxed{}$

$8 + 2 - 3 - 7 = \boxed{}$

$10 - 9 + 1 + 8 = \boxed{}$

$4 + 4 + 0 - 7 = \boxed{}$

$9 - 4 - 5 + 10 = \boxed{}$

Write the answer

$2 + 8 - 4 + 3 = \boxed{}$

$10 - 10 + 10 - 10 = \boxed{}$

$8 + 2 - 8 - 2 = \boxed{}$

$9 - 8 + 1 + 7 = \boxed{}$

$2 + 2 + 2 - 6 = \boxed{}$

$8 - 4 - 4 + 10 = \boxed{}$

Fill in the missing number

2 + ☐ − 2 = 3

☐ − 4 + 5 = 5

2 + ☐ − 4 = 0

5 − 2 + ☐ = 4

1 − ☐ + 0 = 1

☐ + 0 − 0 = 2

Fill in the missing number

6 + ☐ − 4 = 5

7 − ☐ + 3 = 6

3 + 0 − ☐ = 0

8 − ☐ + 1 = 7

☐ − 4 + 6 = 7

☐ + 2 − 3 = 6

Fill in the missing number

$$7 + 3 - \boxed{} = 7$$

$$\boxed{} - 4 + 4 = 8$$

$$8 + \boxed{} - 0 = 8$$

$$1 - 1 + \boxed{} = 1$$

$$\boxed{} - 5 + 5 = 5$$

$$\boxed{} + 9 - 3 = 7$$

Fill in the missing number

1 + ☐ − 1 = 9

7 − 6 + ☐ = 5

2 + ☐ − 0 = 10

10 − 9 + ☐ = 2

☐ − 3 + 5 = 8

4 + ☐ − 1 = 9

Fill in the missing number

$$\boxed{} + \boxed{8} - \boxed{} = \boxed{8}$$

$$\boxed{} - \boxed{} + \boxed{1} = \boxed{7}$$

$$\boxed{9} + \boxed{} - \boxed{} = \boxed{9}$$

$$\boxed{} - \boxed{0} + \boxed{} = \boxed{8}$$

$$\boxed{} - \boxed{} + \boxed{2} = \boxed{6}$$

$$\boxed{} + \boxed{} - \boxed{1} = \boxed{9}$$

Fill in the missing number

1 + 8 - ☐ + 2 = 6

3 - ☐ + 4 - 5 = 1

4 + 3 - 5 - ☐ = 0

☐ - 4 + 0 + 7 = 9

3 + ☐ + 2 - 5 = 4

5 - 3 - ☐ + 0 = 0

Fill in the missing number

$4 + \boxed{} - 3 + 2 = 7$

$8 - 5 + \boxed{} - 5 = 2$

$7 + 3 - 5 - \boxed{} = 1$

$8 - \boxed{} + 6 + 1 = 8$

$4 + 3 + \boxed{} - 6 = 3$

$10 - \boxed{} - 5 + 5 = 9$

Fill in the missing number

| $\boxed{}$ | + | $\boxed{8}$ | - | $\boxed{5}$ | + | $\boxed{2}$ | = | $\boxed{5}$ |

| $\boxed{9}$ | - | $\boxed{7}$ | + | $\boxed{}$ | - | $\boxed{5}$ | = | $\boxed{3}$ |

| $\boxed{6}$ | + | $\boxed{2}$ | - | $\boxed{8}$ | - | $\boxed{}$ | = | $\boxed{0}$ |

| $\boxed{7}$ | - | $\boxed{7}$ | + | $\boxed{}$ | + | $\boxed{1}$ | = | $\boxed{6}$ |

| $\boxed{3}$ | + | $\boxed{3}$ | + | $\boxed{3}$ | - | $\boxed{}$ | = | $\boxed{0}$ |

| $\boxed{2}$ | - | $\boxed{}$ | - | $\boxed{1}$ | + | $\boxed{1}$ | = | $\boxed{1}$ |

Fill in the missing number

$10 + \boxed{} - 10 + \boxed{} = 10$

$9 - \boxed{} + 9 - 9 = 0$

$8 + \boxed{} - \boxed{} - 2 = 0$

$\boxed{} - 4 + 5 + \boxed{} = 7$

$8 + \boxed{} + 2 - \boxed{} = 1$

$\boxed{} - \boxed{} - 2 + 9 = 9$

Fill in the missing number

6 + ☐ - 8 + ☐ = 10

7 - ☐ + 6 - 7 = 0

☐ + ☐ - ☐ - 1 = 1

7 - ☐ + ☐ + 0 = 8

☐ + ☐ + ☐ - ☐ = 4

0 - ☐ - ☐ + 0 = 0

Think of six ways to make 7

9 + ☐ − ☐ + ☐ = 7

☐ − ☐ + ☐ − 3 = 7

☐ + 8 − ☐ − ☐ = 7

☐ − ☐ + 5 + ☐ = 7

☐ + 1 + ☐ − ☐ = 7

☐ − 0 − ☐ + ☐ = 7

Think of six ways to make 8

[ ] + 5 - [ ] + [ ] = 8

[ ] - [ ] + [ ] - 1 = 8

[ ] + [ ] - 3 - [ ] = 8

[ ] - 2 + [ ] + [ ] = 8

[ ] + [ ] + [ ] - [ ] = 8

[ ] - [ ] - [ ] + [ ] = 8

Think of six ways to make 9

☐ + ☐ − ☐ + 2 = 9
☐ − ☐ + ☐ − 1 = 9
9 + ☐ − ☐ − ☐ = 9
☐ − 10 + ☐ + ☐ = 9
☐ + ☐ + ☐ − ☐ = 9
☐ − ☐ − ☐ + ☐ = 9

Think of six ways to make 10

$\boxed{}$ + $\boxed{}$ - $\boxed{}$ + $\boxed{5}$ = $\boxed{10}$

$\boxed{}$ - $\boxed{8}$ + $\boxed{}$ - $\boxed{}$ = $\boxed{10}$

$\boxed{}$ + $\boxed{10}$ - $\boxed{}$ - $\boxed{}$ = $\boxed{10}$

$\boxed{}$ - $\boxed{10}$ + $\boxed{}$ + $\boxed{}$ = $\boxed{10}$

$\boxed{}$ + $\boxed{}$ + $\boxed{}$ - $\boxed{}$ = $\boxed{10}$

$\boxed{}$ - $\boxed{}$ - $\boxed{}$ + $\boxed{}$ = $\boxed{10}$

Comparing Numbers

Compare with >,< or =

Tick the box under biggest object and cross out the box under smallest object in each group

Write the correct sign < or >

3	◯	10	3	◯	1
6	◯	4	8	◯	12
12	◯	17	20	◯	19
10	◯	15	13	◯	18
11	◯	9	17	◯	14
14	◯	18	16	◯	20

Geometry

What is the name of this 3D solid?

Circle the correct answer

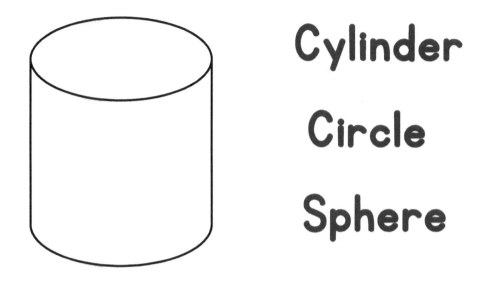

Cylinder

Circle

Sphere

What is the name of this 2D shape?

Circle the correct answer

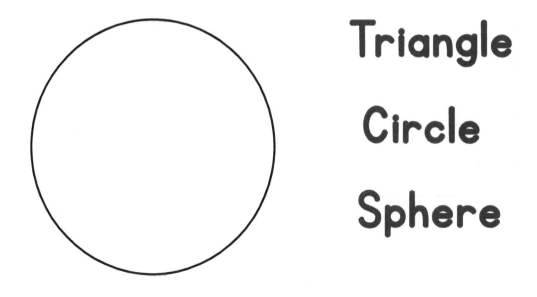

Triangle

Circle

Sphere

What is the name of this 3D solid?
Circle the correct answer

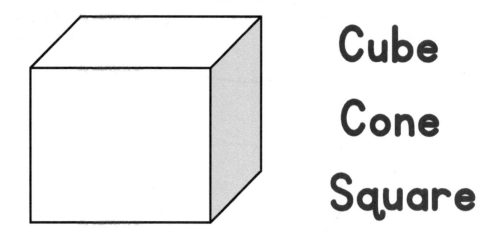

Cube

Cone

Square

What is the name of this 2D shape?
Circle the correct answer

Cube

Rectangle

Square

What is the name of this 3D solid?
Circle the correct answer

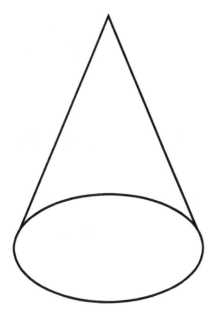

Trapezoid
Cone
Cylinder

What is the name of this 2D shape?
Circle the correct answer

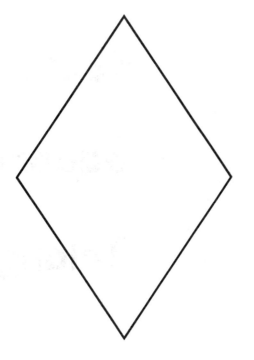

Cone

Rhombus

Sphere

What is the name of this 3D solid?
Circle the correct answer

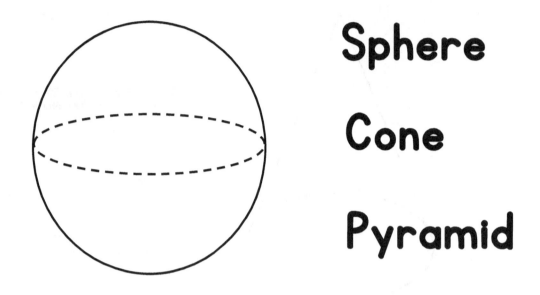

Sphere

Cone

Pyramid

What is the name of this 2D shape?
Circle the correct answer

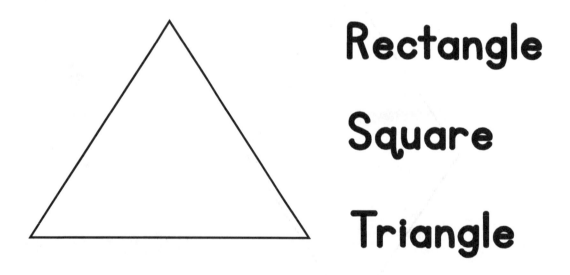

Rectangle

Square

Triangle

What is the name of this 3D solid?
Circle the correct answer

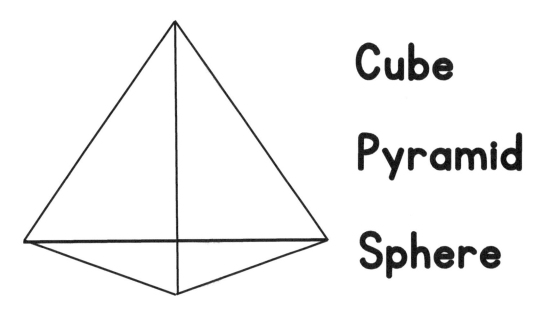

Cube

Pyramid

Sphere

What is the name of this 2D shape?
Circle the correct answer

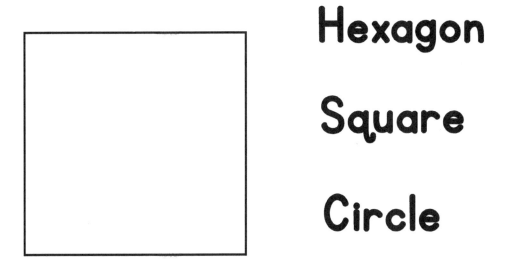

Hexagon

Square

Circle

Made in United States
Troutdale, OR
04/09/2024

19070955R00051